The Concept of NO....

How to Take Responsibility and Let Your No BE No

By Gary Czarnecki, MBM

"The Concept of No"

Copyright 2016 Gary M. Czarnecki, MBM

Published by Czar Capital Trading LLC

All rights reserved. No part of this book may be reproduced (except for inclusion in reviews), disseminated or utilized in any form or by any means, electronic or mechanical, including photocopying, recording, or in any information storage and retrieval system, or Internet/World Wide Web without written permission from the author or publisher.

Printed in the United States

Gary M. Czarnecki

1. Biography/Inspirational/Motivational

Contents

Preface: Introduction to "NO"

Chapter 1: What are you talking about?

Chapter 2: Take Responsibility or Grow Up

Chapter 3: The concept of Change

Chapter 4: The Consequences of not saying NO

Chapter 5: No Pain, No Gain: Face the Pain of Saying No

Chapter 6: Gratification Elimination

Chapter 7: Trust: Do others trust you to say no?

Chapter 8: Say NO, Save Time

Chapter 9: Saying No to People

Chapter 10: Six steps to saying no

Introduction to "NO"

Before we get into the meat of the message, I would like to give you a bit of encouragement in this process. The contents of this book are not always easy to hear, and it applies to many situations in life that can cause or have already caused a lot of pain. We all have different backgrounds. Most of us have adopted the good as well as the bad traits that perhaps we saw at home growing up or by way of other influences in our lives. Many of you reading this will be able to easily see how the absence of the *concept of no* has caused serious pain in your life or perhaps in someone else's life.

Have you made mistakes in your life? It's time to forget about them! I have too. We all have. This is not about how many mistakes or what type of mistakes you've made. This is about getting to a point in your life where you are ready, willing, and able to pursue change in yourself, regardless of how painful that change may be. It's about getting to a point when you recognize that the biggest problem in your life is none other than you, regardless of what others have done to you.

With that said, I'd like to take this time to tell you that you do, in fact, have greatness within you. However, you can be better. Would you agree with that? I know I can certainly say that about myself on a daily basis. You are far more valuable than you can ever begin to fully understand. God Almighty hand-crafted you and loves you enough to bring you to this point. You are worth the effort and the challenge of change. However, the choice is yours and yours alone.

So, <u>get up</u> from whatever emotional or mental collapse you may be going through, and continue on! You are not a failure for falling down. You are only a failure for staying down. Personal change is never an easy process, but you can change. The sun will shine again and things will get better. If you are serious about making changes in your life, you are already on the right track.

"Everyone thinks of changing the world, but no on thinks of changing himself."

-Leo Tolstoy

Chapter 1: What are you talking about?

There I was, eighteen years old, a senior in high school pulling cooked pizzas out of a hot oven and desperately wanting to take a bite, but I said no. Over and over again, I just had to say no. Instead, I would go to the back of the room, fill up a shaker cup with some cold water, drop in some protein powder and take a swig. I would have to quickly return to the pizza line and continue to watch each pizza until the cheese turned golden-brown prior to pulling them out of the oven and cutting them up.

I can hear you now as you read this. What are you talking about? Most people, as I'm sure you're wondering, would ask themselves why I would choose to not even take a bite. It's just pizza, right? I mean, who cares? No matter how intense the desire to have even one bite of pizza was, I kept saying no. My coworkers at the pizza place could not understand *how* I could say no, but they did understand *why*.

It was the year 2000, my senior year in high school, when I chose to prepare and compete in my first competitive bodybuilding show. I was a former soccer player up to this point, so this competition was a bit different. Rather than relying on a team for success, I quickly realized that in bodybuilding, no one was responsible for my success (or failure) other than me. That was a bit nerve-wracking from day one as I realized that not only was I going to be standing in front of thousands of people wearing almost nothing, but I also had to perform a solo posing routine to music during the evening show--a daunting task for a very shy teenager.

Let me ask you a question: If you were in that situation, would you be tempted to take a bite of pizza when you were at work? How tempted do you think you would be knowing that every bite of pizza you took during that time would be very evident to all five thousand spectators who would watch you onstage in a few months?

Life experience has taught me one of the most powerful concepts, the *concept of no*. Conversely, it's also one of the most difficult words in life to execute on. Why is that? I've been through many life scenarios and I have built relationships with many people along the way. Looking back, I recognize that not being able to say no in life has been a constant in one way or another for everyone. I was raised by parents who instilled a very strong work ethic in me and my brother and I've been taught to never expect anything in life. The word no came into play over and over again from my parents. "Nobody owes you anything," my father would say. While I would get angry with them as a kid over this, I've come to appreciate them saying no to me so many times. Not that they didn't ever say yes, but you understand what I'm saying. As I've grown to the man that I am now, I can't help but look around me and wonder why we as individuals have become so weak when it comes to standing our ground on important issues. Sounds harsh, I know, but I just cannot understand why it is that our society and generation continues to move backward in terms of daily choices, mindsets, and attitudes.

I have no idea who will end up reading this book, where it will be sold, or if it will ever end up as a New York Times Best-Seller. I'm writing this book because God has given me a level of discipline and strength that most people envy. But should they really envy it, or can anyone have the discipline needed to make better choices in life? I do not write this book in any self-righteous way. In fact, I personally continue to struggle to exercise this discipline and make wise choices in various areas in my life. It will always be a process for all of us. The point here is not to preach to you or to make you feel bad about past or present choices that you've made. We all have made poor decisions in our lives, no matter how big or small, myself included. This is designed to be a short read--a few hard-hitting truths that we all need to hear and remind ourselves of every day. The only objective here is for this book to be a resource and encouragement to you *if* you begin by making a choice to self-reflect and analyze your own behavior as it relates to the choices you make.

With that said, **STOP READING**, put the book down, and in genuine humility, take this time to think through the choices you have made in the past and all of the little choices you make daily. Honestly, what needs to change in your life?

Chapter 2: Take Responsibility or Grow Up

A topic such as this cannot be discussed effectively without beginning the process with some tough things to say and to admit. Unfortunately, this is typically the biggest sticking point for most people because it points the finger in only one direction--right at them. Even some of the most seasoned individuals in life have developed the daily choice to avoid responsibility for their actions. I've seen it countless times and I'm sure you have too. Are you that person? If I had a dollar for every time I've heard an overweight or unhealthy person tell me that they are too busy to exercise... Is that you?

Here's my point: no matter what you are going through, no matter where you are in your life, <u>you</u> are responsible. There will always be people and situations in your life that you cannot control, but your response and behavior to all of it is your responsibility alone. Stop blaming your boss, your parents, your spouse, your children, etc. **Your choices determine your fate.**

So how can you come to this conclusion? Simple--grow up. The concept of "growing up" really has very little to do with getting older. Growing up (or failing to) is all about your personal, emotional, mental, and spiritual growth as a result of your life experiences. I have seen two types of people in my life. One is the person who has experienced a lot and chose to get better in life rather than get bitter in life. This person is a wealth of knowledge and wisdom and surprisingly, they can be in their nineties or in their twenties. The other is the person who chooses to do the exact opposite. Life has happened to them, which can be very difficult, but they made the choice to avoid taking responsibility for their behavior, thinking, and overall response to the blows that life has given them. Which person are you?

Have you gone through a divorce or breakup and came to the conclusion that it's all the other person's fault? Did you go off on your wife or husband and disrespect them with your words because they did this or that? Are you unhappy with how you look and feel, but you're just too busy to change your lifestyle and eating habits? Have you managed to save zero dollars because you just do not make enough money, or is it because you chose to spend what you earn foolishly? I can ask a thousand of these types of questions, because I've asked them all of myself at one time or another.

This is the perfect opportunity for you to once again take a step back in humility and honestly analyze your own choices and behaviors in whatever it is that you are going through, went through, or want to change in your life. One thing is for sure, the only thing in this world that you can change is yourself. Nothing will be different in your life until you think differently about yourself and your circumstances. Therefore, choose this very minute to acknowledge that you are responsible for where you are in life and the consequences of the choices you've made in your life. No matter what another person has said or done to you, you alone need to assess your behavior and take responsibility. After reading this chapter, if you still will not accept this truth and you still think that other people and circumstances are the problem, there is only one thing left to say to you…You need to grow up! Consider this "tough love." It's time to stop thinking like a child and to begin thinking like an adult.

Chapter 3: The Concept of Change

As we move into some deeper discussion on this principle, it becomes very important to embrace the changes that need to occur in your life if you are going to move forward. The difficult part in being better in anything is when we come to the point where we must choose to accept the uncomfortable feeling that comes along with moving in another direction. This is what embracing change is really all about. It's one thing to mentally acknowledge that you need to make some changes. It's another thing entirely to act on making the changes whole-heartedly while fully understanding the level of discomfort that will come along with them.

If it makes you feel any better, change is something that most of us struggle with. Some are stuck in a paradigm way of thinking or behavior and absolutely dread any shift in that paradigm. In reality, though, the change itself is not what we fear, but rather the discomfort that comes along with it. With that said, change itself requires *the concept of no* to avoid the negative behavior or thinking that causes us to run away from discomfort. It's interesting when you think about it, because all of us consciously know that pain and discomfort is necessary for change. So why is it that so few are willing to face it head-on? If pain and discomfort typically result in such great changes within us, why aren't we running toward it and welcoming the pain? I think about this truth in my own life as I seek to embrace this concept daily. I think of the big and little things in my life that I failed to say no to, and struggle to understand why that occurred. Society tells us every day that we should be comfortable and life should be easy. So buy this or buy that and life will be easier, right? Unfortunately, life only gets more difficult with this mindset, as there is no "quick fix" or "easy life." It is only in the times of controversy and pain that we can actually grow. There is no need to grow when the bills are all paid and there's a Ferrari in the driveway. Our thinking and perspective change only when we have gone <u>completely</u> through tough times and have grown in our maturity as a result. Personally, I can look back and see all of the trials and difficult times that God allowed me to experience to bring me to this point. I can also say that I still have long way to go. One of the easiest ways to grow in life is to look back at situations in your life and see how far you've come, but then ask yourself, "Am I better as a result? What did I learn in the process that I can carry forward into the future?" That is true change. The point of this chapter is to encourage you to look back at your life and visualize how your past has shaped you to who you are now, whether good or bad. *The minute we forget what we've gone through and what we've learned as a result is the minute we have failed to change.*

Chapter 4: The Consequences of NOT saying no

If you have made the choice to take personal responsibility for your choices, even if that meant growing up in your thinking, CONGRATULATIONS! You've taken the first step to not only making better choices, but to begin to implement the *concept of no*. If you have genuinely come to the place of humility in this area, please understand that it takes time to completely change the way we think on that. You have certainly taken the first step, but self-reflection is much like a muscle that needs to be exercised over time in order to grow and to become a consistent part of your life. So keep it up!

Funny, isn't it? We look back on our lives after certain situations have played out, and wonder why we didn't say no to something a long time ago. We typically wonder why things ended up the way they did. I cannot even begin to tell you how many times I've wondered that, even within the last six months. Why didn't I end that relationship sooner? Why didn't I start saving money a long time ago? Why/how could allow myself get so out of shape? The questions of "why" are endless, but it's far more important to channel the question of "why" toward yourself rather than someone or something else. I can remember the times when I sat in the pain of a broken relationship or financial struggles, wondering how I got there and then defaulting to thoughts of how foolish my ex(s) were and how they messed up the relationship or how my small income was for the reason I had no money in the bank. I finally got to a point in my life when I realized that my own thought process and perspective were the problem. It was time for me to stop listening to my own advice. Despite the fact that my ex(s) were also loaded with faults and certainly did largely contribute to the failed relationship, I realized that I would never be able to control or change another person nor would I always be able to change my circumstances. So that left me with only one conclusion. It was time to begin taking responsibility for my actions, thoughts, words, and behaviors that had been exposed in these situations.

Story time. I got married at an early age and entered into a life-long relationship with someone who was really only supposed to be in my life for a season. Of course, I didn't see that back then, but I will never forget the first two years of that relationship. After our marriage, the relationship quickly began to decline. I was so disappointed with her never taking part in the relationship at an adult level. As a result of her behavior in the relationship, I would routinely yell at her, using very poor word choices. I never encouraged her and I became cold, bitter, and distant--so much so that I wouldn't even kiss her. I held this callous attitude and I chose to implement a conditional love where if she would continue to refuse to help me with the house, bills, and other responsibilities, I wouldn't give her a kiss. How childish is that? In case you're wondering, this was the time when a friend of mine bluntly told me to grow up.

A year and a half in, and she separates from me and tells me that she wants a divorce. Whack! It was like being hit in the head with a hammer. I strongly believe it was God communicating with me to bring me to a point of humility and responsibility. She was wrong in a lot of ways in that relationship, but my eyes were opened to the fact that my choices and behavior were the real culprit. Why? Well, I quickly realized that until I take responsibility for my own actions, I cannot expect others to do the same. Whether they do the same or not, my character (or lack thereof) becomes crystal clear at this point. That is a major concept in leadership that I quickly learned as a result. She was always completely responsible for her behavior, but I had absolutely zero control over what she chose to do. I only had control over myself. I learned that the biggest problem in my marriage was me. Had I chosen to think and act differently in response to her behavior, the relationship would not have gotten to rock-bottom so quickly. As a result of this new awakening, I immediately set up a time to get counseling; she followed suit and the relationship was slowly restored. Even though the relationship ended many years later, I can still hold my head up, knowing that I never made that mistake again. Does this sound familiar in any way in your own life?

This is where the word no begins to come into play. When people or life circumstances disappoint, as they are sure to do, you must take a step back and say no to the thinking and attitudes that create the negative consequences in life. I strongly believe that had I said no to the immature attitude and conditional love toward my wife, the consequences of my rock-bottom position would not have existed. It was only when I finally said no to my poor way of thinking that the relationship began to move in the right direction.

Now, I would also add that this particular outcome is never guaranteed. Saying no to destructive behaviors, words, attitudes, etc. is not something you only implement to change the outcome of a given situation. Rather, it is the only way to avoid the pain of consequences. How many times have you experienced pain because you failed to say no to something? The *concept of no* is something that can help you to choose only the best in your life by eliminating everything that is less than the best. Whether it's the friends you hang out with, the romantic relationships you choose to be involved in, or saying no daily to the garbage food that keeps you from being healthy, the consequences of <u>not</u> saying no should be your primary motivator for saying it.

So how does this look in practice? Here's a very simple example. I'm craving Chinese food as I write this--a big weakness for your humble author. There's a place right down the street with the best crab ragoon, and they deliver. Though I am very tempted, I'm choosing to say no. Not because I want to sound credible here, but because if I order Chinese food right now, I will lose about twenty dollars out of my allocated food budget for the week--way too much for one meal. Additionally, I will have added a substantial amount of calories to my diet today, which basically eliminates the thirty minutes of cardio I did this morning Additionally, I will need to do cardio again tomorrow morning. No thanks.

In this situation, my bad behavior is ordering Chinese because of a sudden urge to do so. You will also notice that there are three times as many consequences as benefits in this situation.

So how do you begin to say no to bad habits and behaviors? It is simple in theory, yet difficult in practice. You <u>think of the consequences of NOT saying no</u>. That is how you will be able to slowly begin to strengthen your avoidance of behaviors that lead to negative consequences. When you begin to realize that the consequences of the decision outweigh the benefits, the urge to do the behavior will begin to diminish. The next time you are faced with a decision like my Chinese food example, no matter how small, I challenge you to focus on the negative outcomes rather than the short-term gratification.

Chapter 5: No Pain, No Gain: Face the Pain of saying No

Another tough topic for discussion. You and I both know that we fail to say no because doing so will typically result in some type of pain or deferred pleasure. Life experience has taught me that the only way to make forward progress in life is to face the very pain that we all try to avoid. This chapter, while short, is pivotal in terms of learning to say no. Why is it that so many people today fail to grow mentally, emotionally, and spiritually? You guessed it: because they refuse to face the pain. As soon as something is no longer comfortable, they run the other direction at 100 MPH and make excuses for why.

We have all been at the pool or at the beach on a hot day. You glance at the blue water (hopefully it's blue) and you cannot wait for the cool refreshment of being completely immersed. There's a problem, though. You dip your toe in the water and begin to have second thoughts, as the water seems to be freezing. Think back to the last time you were in that situation. Did you go home after dipping your toe in the water? Did you choose to "work on your tan" on the side of the pool? Of course not. You forced yourself to face the temporary discomfort of the feeling of cold water on your body by jumping in. This is a very small example of how we all need to be approaching our quest to say no to the "excuse advisors" in our minds. The temporary discomfort or feeling of missing out quickly vanishes once we put our proverbial foot down and say no.

As the title of this chapter suggests, this simple concept can be compared to the weightlifting slogan, "no pain, no gain." Like a muscle, our ability to say no, which runs parallel to our level of discipline, grows when it is exercised. Looking back to the opening story, I spent many years pouring my heart into my bodybuilding. To be completely honest, though, I do not have the ideal genetics for the sport. I knew that going in, but I didn't care. I saw it as nothing more than a challenge for myself. Due to my upbringing, I have a strong work ethic that I applied to everything I did even in my early years. In every sport I played, I would put in whatever time and energy was necessary to practice and be at my best. Bodybuilding, however, was different than my usual exercise in discipline. Practicing a couple of times per week for soccer was very different. Bodybuilding is a 24-hour sport. Everything you do can and will affect the outcome of your physique. This meant (for me) training twice per day and meal prepping for eight meals per day. Yes, I said eight. This meant meal timing and watching the clock to ensure the proper timing of my meals and nutrition. This also meant ensuring that I was drinking at least one gallon of water per day, all while keeping my carbohydrate content very low, around only twenty complex carbohydrates per meal. With my carbohydrate content so low, it was difficult to focus mentally at times since the brain uses carbohydrates as a source of fuel to function. All of this is to say the only reason I was able to successfully do this (four different shows) was the constant thought of the consequences of failing to exercise my physical muscles as well as the muscles of my discipline.

The point is this: if you want the ability to say no, you must be willing to face the pain of saying no (or delayed gratification). I wish I could recommend a pill you can take to develop this type of emotional discipline, but there simply is no other way. You must be willing to recognize and delay the gratification each and every time, regardless of how small the decision is. You must get to the place where you are fed up with the pain of your decisions and realize that it's less painful to face them head-on.

I recently had a messaging exchange with a classmate where the topic was about trusting teammates. She was vulnerable in sharing her issues with trust over the years because of all kinds of abuse that she endured both as a child and into her adult life. I asked her what changed her thinking on choosing to trust people. Her response was, "At some point it becomes harder to stay in that painful place than to go through the difficulty of changing. That difficulty feels a whole lot better when you know you're doing something good for yourself."

I really took that wisdom to heart, as I recently had a friend who chose to break off an engagement with a woman he had been with for over a year. This particular situation was an opportunity for him to personally practice what I am writing here in a very intense way. This woman had a few qualities that he always longed for in a wife. As time went on, however, he began to realize that they were just not in the same season in life and they would not be able to be on the same page with important topics, behaviors, and lifestyles. Though he genuinely loved her and gave the relationship ample time to be on the same life trajectory, it soon became evident that trying to force her to think and live like he does was just not fair to either of them. Knowing that she was crazy about him, he got to the point where choosing to part ways was less painful than continuing in the relationship. It doesn't always happen overnight, but he finally got to the point where he had to face the pain, observe the long-term consequences of sitting in the pain, and simply say no, regardless of how painful it would be.

You will never get to the place where you can push destructive behaviors aside to focus on doing positive behaviors until you begin to exercise your discipline. Discipline is what enables us to face the fears we have that cause us to feel temporarily lonely, unhappy, or even hungry when we really aren't. It's what enables us to resist sexual temptation, knowing that failure to say no can result in unplanned pregnancy, sexually transmitted diseases, or even just guilt of falling in that way. It's what gives the athlete the strength to choose a nutritious diet, knowing that failure to do so will dampen his or her performance, and it's what gives us the ability to break off relationships (even engagements) that simply are not healthy.

Chapter 6: Gratification Elimination

We've all probably heard the phrase "delayed gratification" before. In fact, I just used this phrase in the previous chapter. It's a vital term that can be applied to many areas in life, including money, eating habits, etc. Have you ever actually given any thought to how you apply delayed gratification in your life? Most of us haven't, and in all reality, it's because the *concept of no* must be applied to adhere to this powerful principle.

One of the most apparent areas where we all should be applying this principle is within our finances. Of course, as with all of these principles, I am guilty as well. However, I can't help but ask why it is so difficult to say no and actually delay gratification. We are so bombarded by advertisements and media that we now are conditioned to want things that we either do not need or shouldn't buy at all. Does this ring true in your life? The statistics are alarming. I recently heard a statistic that basically said that the majority of Americans have less than one thousand dollars saved. It's difficult to accept at first until you really look around at the financial behavior of the masses. Why? Both you and I have been conditioned to not think for ourselves. We are told directly and indirectly from every angle that we need to buy this or that right now "while supplies last."

I write this chapter to propose a new strategy that I would encourage you to implement in your life right now. Rather than only trying to practice delayed gratification, try practicing "gratification elimination." The *concept of no* is designed to give you the tools and mindset necessary to eliminate things, behaviors, and patterns of thinking that do not need to be delayed. They actually need to be ELIMINATED altogether. Why defer something that you don't need at all? Why not remove the desire to do something (or not do something constructive) that is destructive altogether? Don't get me wrong. Delayed gratification is a very important and wise principle that applies to many things in life including buying a home, a car, or even choosing what school to go to. It helps us to not make emotional decisions, to slow down and wait. It enables us to force ourselves to think thoroughly through an important decision rather than foolishly move forward only because it's on sale or because our emotions are running rampant. Gratification elimination is vital to the *concept of no* because it enables you to remove whatever it is that you are desiring so much.

Most of us who have gone through a breakup have struggled with this very concept shortly after the breakup. He or she has to swing by to pick up personal belongings left at your house. Or it's your ex-husband or ex-wife and you have to see each other to swap time with the kids. While you cannot escape seeing this person, you certainly do have control over the context in which you see them. I've known many people who end up putting themselves in a situation where their emotions and newfound realization of the upcoming loneliness kicks in and the next thing they know they are seriously regretting what happened when they saw their ex.

My point is this: slow down and think. Think through the desire at hand and run away from it altogether if at all possible. If you were on a strict diet and trying to lose weight, would you go hang out at McDonalds? Why do we make such dumb decisions in this regard? <u>Eliminate the gratification</u>. Don't naively rationalize about how it'll be ok and you will stand your ground. Be smart and don't put yourself in that position to begin with. Why create your own pain? Commit yourself to eliminating the circumstances that breed the desires and behaviors that cause you the very pain you come to regret.

Chapter 7: Selfishness: Can others trust you to say no?

This may come as a news flash to some of you, but your ability to say no in your life is not only about you. Though the principles in this book will clearly impact your well-being and personal growth, in reality, your ability (or lack thereof) to implement the concepts in this book strongly affects others in your life.

Think about a time when you failed to say no to a negative behavior or when you did say no to a positive behavior. Whether big or small, an acute or chronic pattern, how did it affect you? Now let me ask you another question: how did that same situation affect those around you? In what way did it hurt or impact someone else? Take a few minutes to honestly think through and answer that question. Did it hurt your spouse in some way? Did it take valuable time away from your kids? Did it send a very negative message to someone you know?

You know, most of us go through life thinking that our life, decisions, and behaviors are all about us as individuals. We all make decisions in our careers, relationships, financially, and in many other ways without giving even one thought to the macro-effect on those in our lives. This is not to say that there aren't times in our lives when the wise decision may be unpopular among those in our lives. We make many decisions that are all about our selfish desires rather than how those decisions may impact others. There are many people in this world who choose to uproot their families to follow a specific job or career path while simultaneously pulling their spouses and children away from friends, family, and other important relationships, all in the name of "providing for the family." While there is nothing foundationally wrong with the underlying issue of relocating for a job, the larger question that goes unanswered time and time again is, "How will this affect those around me?"

I have also seen this concept play out as it relates to one's own physical health. For some reason, many of us get married and then lose all drive to continue to take care of ourselves physically. Maybe it's getting comfortable knowing your spouse loves you no matter what or perhaps just an increased level of stress in life. Call it what you will, but allow me to provide a different view on this scenario. While it may seem counterintuitive, your physical health affects those around you. Failing to take care of your own health leads to stress, worry, and unnecessary anxiety for your family, spouse, and friends. Have you ever had a friend or family member struggling with a serious health issue? How did it make you feel? Were you at all concerned about who was going to win the Super Bowl or World Series when you found out about the health problems of your loved one? Of course not. The fear of "what if" suddenly entered your heart and mind as well.

There are many other similar situations or behaviors that can be applied here, but I want you to understand that <u>you are not your own</u> and the decisions you make on behalf of yourself may drag others into the consequences of those actions. Consider those around you and never neglect the pain that you may be causing others in the midst of your daily decision-making.

Chapter 8: Say NO, Save TIME

I've heard it time and time again. "I don't have time to get to the gym" and other excuses for why we don't make the right choices. Unbeknownst to most is that the best way to free up time in our lives is by way of the *concept of no*. Growing and bettering ourselves in anything requires prioritizing our daily tasks. There are countless distractions and mental leeches that cling to us that we must say no to if we are to grow in this area. One of the most obvious is television. I've always wondered what type of a culture we would be if TV for entertainment purposes didn't exist. It's no wonder marriages are failing left and right when you look at what people spend their time watching--shows that create a false picture of what relationships, marriage or otherwise, actually are. Garbage in, garbage out. Men and women spend so much time watching fabricated relationships that resemble a fairy tale that they begin to expect the same in real life. Selfishness runs rampant and expectations become so out of whack that no real person can even begin to measure up. The media has become the biggest influencer in most peoples' lives. While I'm not suggesting that all TV is bad, what I am saying is that the inability to say no to too much TV results in a dampening of our minds, objectivity, and creativity. If people were to eliminate the countless hours they spend in front of the television and instead began to read thought-provoking growth material, society as a whole would be very different. Wouldn't you agree?

Another example of this is video games. Again, I'm not suggesting that playing video games is wrong, but how much actual time do kids and adults spend in these virtual escapes from reality? If you want to make progress growing personally and professionally, learn to <u>say no</u> to the brain-drain activities that have become standard procedure in your life. Listen to personal development seminars, read books on communication or leadership, spend time talking with people who are smarter than you and challenge your thinking. By saying no to these mind-numbing activities, we are able to create time that we *thought* we didn't have. Think about it for a minute. What daily or weekly activities can you say no to today? In what ways can you eliminate time-wasting activities and replace them with activities that sharpen you?

Chapter 9: Saying No to People

We all have people in our lives that we look up to and respect. For many it's their mother, father, or another family member. For others it's a friend or mentor that has touched them in some way. Regardless of the relationship dynamics, have you ever thought about why you respect them so much? The answer to that is typically a pretty easy one; otherwise you probably wouldn't have so much respect for them. These are the people in our lives that leave a lasting impact. While it's fairly easy to recognize these people in our lives, most of us struggle to look closely at the *other* relationships in our lives. I have learned that it is true that most people come into our lives for only a season. However, many times we attempt to keep these people in our lives longer than they should be. It's really something that only time will show us, but we default to the mentality that we should over-invest in some of these relationships. The important thing to recognize is that it's the <u>quality</u> of the people in our lives, <u>not the</u>

<u>quantity</u> of time that really matters. It's not all that important how long someone is in your life, but rather the way they influence you that really matters (or vice versa). Regardless, it's safe to say that our ability (or inability) to say no in life is greatly influenced by those whom we spend time with. It's been said that we are all a product of the five people in our lives that we spend the most time with. I couldn't agree more.

The question then becomes, who are you spending most of your time with? Leveraging an earlier chapter, you'll recall the discussion about the two types of people that you'll typically experience in life: those who take responsibility and choose to grow from life's struggles, and those who shift the responsibility to everyone else and their circumstances. Earlier, I asked you which one of these people you more closely resemble. Using those same two types of people, let me ask you this: which of those two types of people do you spend the most time with?

Our ability to grow and to say no to destructive behaviors in life is greatly impacted by those around us. The reality is, you may not be a skunk, but if you hang out with skunks, you are going to smell like one anyway. Never underestimate the people around you. Take a close look at your inner circle. Are these people challenging you in any way? Do they speak truth in your life? Do they encourage you to live with integrity, or do they give you a prime example of how not to live? As you work through the *concept of no,* you will begin to see that your ability to grow in this concept and in many other ways will be greatly helped or greatly hindered by those around you. Never settle in your closest relationships. This does not mean you should not get to know or spend zero time with people who do not challenge you. In fact, the quickest way to grow and become smart is to learn from other people's mistakes, whether they learned from them or not. A good friend of mine once told me, "People learned a lot from Forrest Gump, the dumbest of them all." How true is that? While we can learn a lot from the ignorant people in our lives, and we should, wisdom tells us not to spend too much time with them or we will begin to adopt their habits and lifestyle. Unfortunately, many of us have family that fall into this category. While you cannot choose your family members and you should always demonstrate discerning love to them, the concept of limiting your exposure to the negative people in your life should also be implemented in family. Learn to discern what you should and should not share with certain family members. Your path of growth depends upon it. Always be aware of those around you and the impact that they can have in your life. <u>Never</u> settle in this area. On your journey to say no, you must also say no to destructive influences and people in your life. *We must be cognizant of those who will be a resource and asset for making the right choices in life and those who continually make the choices we should steer clear of.*

Chapter 10: Six steps to saying 'NO"

If you've been honest with yourself to this point, I'm sure you are easily able to recognize areas in your thinking that need improvement. So how do we begin to habitually say no? Well, I will be the first to tell you that it is not easy, but I will also be the first to tell you that anything worth doing in life is never easy. With that said, let's analyze six practical steps that will begin to move you in the right direction.

Step 1: Admit the Need for Change

As was the topic of chapter two, we have come full-circle to where real change requires humility. Step one requires taking a step back and coming to the realization that the biggest problem in your life is you and you alone. Your perspective, attitude, and reaction to what happens to you, regardless of what others have done to you, is all under your control. Therefore, I would suggest that you do not move forward in this process until you have fully come to this realization and you are ready to admit your failures and fully take responsibility for them. It is also important to see the bigger picture regarding your future. The worst thing you can do going forward would be to roll over poor behaviors and thinking into future relationships, jobs, etc. Have you come to this realization yet? I sincerely hope you have.

Step 2: Recognize the Opportunity to Say NO

It amazes me, even in my own life, how many times we consciously know what path to take when faced with the opportunity to say no, yet we fail to say no. Can I assume you can relate? Well, knowing what direction to take in these situations, big or small, is only part of the equation. The first step is to <u>recognize in the moment</u> when you are in a position to exercise this discipline. Just last week I was in line at the grocery store waiting to check out. Of course, as all clever merchandisers do, this store had numerous impulse items at the counter for me to grab, one of which was one of my favorite auto air fresheners. Now, obviously there is nothing wrong with purchasing an air freshener for my car. However, rather than grab it off the shelf, I was able to slow down and remember my own advice: *the concept of no*. Did I need it? No. Then why would I buy it? Interesting thought, right? Unable to answer that question, I chose to take a pass. A very small example, but you can see how simply and how often we are faced with opportunities to say no. It's when we say yes to all of these small things that we develop the inability to say no to the bigger things in life. As we discussed in earlier chapters, discipline is like a muscle that needs to be strengthened. Like a muscle, it will require some short-term pain to do. Always be conscious of the little opportunities for you to say no.

Step 3: Ponder the Consequences

Again, circling back to an earlier chapter, our ability to say no can be greatly increased by simply pondering the consequences of the action or behavior. Remember the Chinese food example I gave you in chapter four? How was I able to say no to ordering the food? I flipped the thought of how delicious it would be to satisfy that hunger craving over to the consequences of my ordering the food. These included the wasted exercise I did that very morning, having to redo the cardio in the morning, and the big chunk that would be taken out of my food budget for only one meal. By focusing on the consequences, I was able to literally eliminate that very craving. You can too! It's amazing how quickly these desires vanish when we think about the consequences and how the outcomes far outweigh the temporary pleasure we would get.

Step 4: Face the Desire Head-On

You will see that step four instantaneously follows step three. When you ponder the consequences, you will immediately be faced with the pain and frustration of not gratifying that desire. <u>Stay strong</u> in this moment, as it is the most challenging step in this process. Face it head-on. Once you succeed in this step, it will become easier every time going forward. Remember, there is no gain/growth in life without the pain. So learn to embrace the pain and face it head-on.

Step 5: Replace it with a positive thought or behavior

Once you have faced the pain head-on, you now have the opportunity to replace the poor choice with a positive choice. Instead of buying the chocolate cake you keep staring at when at the grocery store, say no and go pick up something healthier that you will also enjoy. Instead of spending the extra fifty dollars you ended up with at the end of the month, send all fifty to your savings account. By the time you get to this step, you've also gotten through the toughest part of the process. You are now free to make a better choice. Do not neglect this opportunity!

Step 6: Be Vulnerable and Be Held Accountable

We were never designed to do life alone. Let's be honest; life is tough. I could never quite understand how people avoid getting close to others. As it relates to the topic at hand and many others, for that matter, making forward progress requires help. If we are honest with ourselves, we can easily see how going it alone becomes self-defeating. For this reason, it becomes incredibly important to be vulnerable with friends and family about your struggle and ask them to hold you accountable. Always be discerning, however, in terms of who you ask. Be sure you are asking someone you can trust in your vulnerability and confidentiality. Ask them to check up with you consistently and hold you accountable for moving forward in this area. You are much more likely to make the right choices when you know someone will be asking about it.

Epilogue

There's no question, we've covered a lot in a short read. While I seriously hope you enjoyed reading *The Concept of No*, I even more sincerely hope that you have begun to think through your own life in this regard and act on the information that you've learned here. The fact is, the only thing in life that you can change is yourself. Powerful truth. Those who embrace it will never be the same. Be the person who is willing to change the world, starting with themselves. You have the ability to change and the ability to say no.

Thank you again for investing the time to read this book. I wish you all the best.

"The unexamined life is not worth living." - Socrates

www.ingramcontent.com/pod-product-compliance
Lightning Source LLC
Chambersburg PA
CBHW061448180526
45170CB00004B/1609